DUDLEY SCHOOLS LIBRARY
AND INFORMATION SERVICE

KU-453-194

Schools Library and Information Services

S00000643807

Orangutans

By Christy Steele

www.raintreepublishers.co.uk

Visit our website to find out more information about Raintree books.

To order:
☎ Phone 44 (0) 1865 888112
▤ Send a fax to 44 (0) 1865 314091
💻 Visit the Raintree Bookshop at www.raintreepublishers.co.uk to browse our catalogue and order online.

First published in Great Britain by Raintree Publishers, Halley Court, Jordan Hill, Oxford, OX2 8EJ, part of Harcourt Education.
Raintree is a registered trademark of Harcourt Education Ltd.

© Harcourt Education Ltd 2003
The moral right of the proprietor has been asserted.

All rights reserved. No part of this publication may be reproduced, stored in a retrieval system, or transmitted in any form or by any means, electronic, mechanical, photocopying, recording, or otherwise, without either the prior written permission of the publishers or a licence permitting restricted copying in the United Kingdom issued by the Copyright Licensing Agency Ltd, 90 Tottenham Court Road, London W1T 4LP (www.cla.co.uk).

Originated by Dot Gradations Ltd
Printed and bound in Hong Kong and China by South China

ISBN 1 844 21091 X
07 06 05 04 03
10 9 8 7 6 5 4 3 2 1

British Library Cataloguing in Publication Data
Steele, Christy
Orangutans - (Animals of the rainforest)
1. Orangutan - Juvenile literature
2. Rain forest ecology - Juvenile literature
I.Title
599.8'83
A catalogue for this book is available from the British Library.

Acknowledgements
The publishers would like to thank the following for permission to reproduce photographs:
Photophile/Roger Holden, pp. **8, 16, 19, 23, 24**; Root Resources/Anthony Mercieca, pp. **4–5**; Visuals Unlimited, Kjell B. Sandved, pp. **1, 15**; C.R. George, pp. **11, 20**; Gary W. Carter, p. **12**; Inga Spence, pp. **27, 28**; Warren Photographic pp. **7, 18**.

Cover photograph by Digital Stock.

Every effort has been made to contact copyright holders of any material reproduced in this book. Any omissions will be rectified in subsequent printings if notice is given to the publishers.

Contents

PUBLIC LIBRARIES

-46657

643807. SOH

JS99.88

Any words appearing in the text in bold, **like this**, are explained in the Glossary.

cheeks
see page 13

arms
see page 14

red hair
see pages 7, 13

hands and feet
see pages 7, 14

MALAYSIA

South
China Sea

MALAYSIA

SUMATRA

BORNEO

Java Sea

JAVA

Range of the orangutan
Surrounding land
Sea
Borders

A quick look at orangutans ·

What do orangutans look like?
Orangutans are large, hairy, red-brown apes. They have long hands, arms and feet.

Where do orangutans live?
Orangutans live in rainforests on the islands of Borneo and Sumatra in south-east Asia.

What do orangutans eat?
Orangutans eat mostly fruit. They also eat leaves, bark and insects when they cannot find enough fruit to eat.

How many orangutans are there?
Only about 25,000 orangutans live in the wild. They are in danger of dying out.

Orangutans are the largest apes living in Asia.

Orangutans in rainforests

Orangutans are **mammals**. A mammal is a **warm-blooded** animal with fur and a backbone. Warm-blooded animals have a body temperature that stays the same even when it is hot or cold outside. Temperature is a measure of heat or cold.

Orangutans are important to life in the rainforest. Rainforests are places where many trees and plants grow close together and lots of rain falls. Orangutans eat many kinds of fruits. Some seeds from the fruits leave their bodies in the form of waste. Waste is what a body does not need or use from food that has been eaten. Some new plants grow from these seeds and the plants spread.

Intelligent animals

Scientists have learnt that orangutans are some of the most intelligent animals. Scientists have taught them to point to shapes or use **sign language** to talk. Sign language is a way of using hand movements to stand for words.

Orangutans make and use simple tools. Wild orangutans use sticks to get seeds out of some fruits. They also put sticks into holes and wait for insects to climb on. They pull the sticks out and eat the insects.

Where orangutans live

There are two places in south-east Asia where orangutans live. One place is the island of Sumatra. Sumatra belongs to Indonesia. The other place orangutans live is on the island of Borneo. Part of Borneo belongs to Indonesia, too. The other part of Borneo belongs to the country of Malaysia.

Most orangutans live near rivers in warm lowland **habitats**. A habitat is a place where an animal or plant usually lives.

Orangutans live in the trees of the rainforest.

This male orangutan has large cheek pads and long, red-brown hair.

Canopy

Orangutans live mostly in the trees of the rainforest. This area of thick leaves and branches is called the forest **canopy**.

The canopy has lower, middle and upper parts. Orangutans live in the lower and middle canopy, from 6 metres to 30 metres above the ground. The upper canopy is about 46 metres above the ground.

What orangutans look like

Orangutans are large apes. Males can grow up to 1.5 metres tall. They may weigh up to 100 kilograms. Females are smaller. They usually weigh up to 54 kilograms.

The orangutan's colouring is different from other kinds of apes. Long, red-brown hair covers their bodies. Most other apes have black hair.

Fully grown male orangutans have large pads growing from their cheeks. They have a **sac** hanging from their necks. A sac is part of an animal or plant that is shaped like a bag.

Male orangutans make a special sound so other males know where they are. Scientists call the sound a **long call**. It sounds like a roar. To make the long call, the male breathes in deeply. When he breathes out, the air makes the loud roaring sound.

Life in trees

An orangutan's body is good for travelling in trees. Orangutans have long, strong arms. Their arms are longer than their legs. Orangutans' hands and feet are long and thin. They have moveable thumbs on their hands. Their fingers and toes can bend and curl around branches.

Orangutans are always moving around the rainforest canopy. They have **home ranges**. A home range is the space where an animal stays most of the time. Orangutans live and find food in their home ranges. Females have smaller home ranges than males.

Orangutans move through the canopy using all four hands and feet at the same time. Three of the four are usually holding on to something. The orangutans pull themselves along like people do when climbing. This way of moving through trees is called **slow clambering**.

This young orangutan is using all its hands and feet to move through the trees.

If there is a lot of space between trees, orangutans swing the trees they are on back and forth. They do this until they can grab hold of the next tree and climb on.

Every night, orangutans bend over small tree branches to build nests to sleep in. They build them anywhere from 9 metres to 26 metres above the ground.

Orangutans eat leaves from plants when they cannot find fruit.

What orangutans eat

Orangutans spend a great deal of time looking for food. They spend 60 to 70 per cent of their day finding, picking and eating fruits, bark, leaves and insects.

Sometimes there is more fruit to be found in the rainforests where orangutans live. This is because of **mast fruiting**. Mast fruiting is when most of the fruit trees grow fruit at the same time. This happens about every three to seven years. Food is easy for orangutans to find at this time.

After mast fruiting, there are often many months with little fruit growth. Food is harder for orangutans to find during these months.

Kinds of food

Scientists have learnt that orangutans eat about 400 different kinds of food. They eat plants most of the time, but will sometimes eat insects.

Orangutans eat mainly fruits and nuts. They eat a lot of durians. A durian is a large, round, green fruit with soft, sweet-tasting insides. It smells horrible and has very long spikes.

Sometimes there is not much fruit in the rainforests. Orangutans must then find bark, leaves and insects to eat.

Orangutans eat so much fruit during mast fruiting that they gain weight. This extra weight is fat. Their bodies turn the fat into energy when there is not much fruit.

An orangutan at the Metrozoo in Miami, Florida, stopped eating. A zookeeper created a special cake made of apples, oranges, bananas, carrots, squash, eggs, monkey biscuits and oatmeal. The orangutan liked the cake so much that it began eating again.

Orangutans spend most of their time finding and eating food.

Young orangutans travel around the rainforest with their mothers.

An orangutan's life cycle

Orangutans do not live together in large groups. Males live alone because they do not get along with other males. Mother orangutans often live with one or two of their young. Sometimes young female orangutans of the same age travel together.

Orangutans come together most during mast fruiting. They also mate most often during mast fruiting. Females have more energy to mate then.

Scientists are not sure how long wild orangutans live. They think that they live for 30 to 45 years. They know that orangutans in zoos can live for up to 50 years.

Mating

Male orangutans are ready to mate when they are about fifteen years old. Then they can mate whenever they find females that are willing to mate with them. Often, females will not mate with a male until his cheek pads are fully grown. This does not happen until the males are about twenty years old.

Female orangutans are ready to mate when they are about twelve years old. The females mate about once every six or seven years.

Young

Female orangutans give birth eight-and-a-half months after mating. At birth, orangutans weigh about 1.8 kilograms. They drink their mothers' milk. For the first few years, young orangutans ride on their mothers while learning how to move about on their own.

Young orangutans live with their mothers. Young orangutans learn how to find and eat fruits, leaves, bark and insects. They also learn how to make nests.

Mother orangutans find food and feed it to their young.

Orangutans leave their mothers when they are ten to twelve years old. Females stay close to their mothers' home ranges. Males often travel far away.

In the Malay language, the word 'orangutan' means person of the forest.

Living with orangutans

Scientists believe orangutans are similar to humans in many ways. They study orangutans to find out what early human ancestors might have been like. An ancestor is a family member who lived a long time ago.

Orangutans are **endangered**. Endangered means all the orangutans could die out if things are not done to protect them and their habitats. Scientists believe there are only about 25,000 orangutans left in the wild.

Orangutans in danger

Orangutans are losing their habitats. Huge fires have burned many kilometres of the rainforest. In 1997, forest fires killed about 1000 orangutans. People are also cutting down many trees in the rainforest. Some want to build homes and plant crops there. Some want to sell the wood.

Hunting also kills many orangutans. In Indonesia and Malaysia, it is against the law to hunt, sell or keep pet orangutans. Many people break the law to make money. Hunters kill mother orangutans and take their young. They sell the young to people who want them for pets.

Over time, orangutans grow too large for their owners to take care of. These orangutans cannot go back to the wild. Their mothers never taught them how to live in the rainforest.

Many orangutans are friendly to people. This is why people want pet orangutans. But orangutans should not be taken from their homes in the rainforest.

These orangutans live in a protected wildlife station.

Saving orangutans

Some people are trying to save orangutans. They have built stations and centres to help them.

At the stations, scientists study wild orangutans. This helps save the rainforest where the stations are located. This is one of the best ways to save parts of the rainforest.

At the centres, workers take care of sick or injured orangutans. They also raise young orangutans whose mothers have died. They teach these animals to live in the wild. People hope these actions will help stop orangutans from dying out.

Glossary

canopy (KAN-uh-pee) thick area of leaves high up in the treetops

endangered in danger of dying out

habitat place where an animal or plant usually lives

home range area in which an animal spends most of its time

long call sound like a roar that male orangutans make

mammal warm-blooded animal that has hair and feeds its young on milk

mast fruiting time during which most fruit trees grow fruit all at the same time

sac animal or plant part that is shaped like a bag

sign language language in which hand movements are used instead of speech

slow clambering way of moving through trees using both hands and both feet

warm-blooded animal that stays at a steady warm temperature

More information

Internet sites

Rainforest Education
www.rainforestlive.org.uk

Orangutan Foundation International
www.orangutan.org

Useful address

Orangutan Foundation UK
7 Kent Terrace,
London,
NW1 4RP

Books to read

Theodorou, R; Telford C. *Amazing Journeys: Up a Rainforest Tree. Heinemann Library, Oxford, 1998*

Index